D0236035

England is a Garden

England is a Garden

Catherine Hamilton

Dedication

To the memory of my mother, who taught me to appreciate the beauty of all flowers.

Acknowledgements

I am deeply grateful to many people throughout England who, by their kindness, friendship, and willingness to share their great love of flowers and magnificent historical heritage, made the work for this book not only possible but an event of great joy.

My special thanks to Anne Barnes, Surrey; Gladys and Michael Beattie, Hertfordshire; Roger and Nicky Burley, Kent; K. F. Brown, Surrey; H. Catling, Gloucestershire; George Kirkby, Cumbria; Lord and Lady Tranmire, Yorkshire; Mary and Tom Cook, Yorkshire; Alan Newton, Hampshire; Dr and Mrs Delap, Cumbria; Miss E. Webb, Warwickshire; Jacquie Spiers, London; Christine Tindall, Kent; Frances Lonsbrough, Cleveland.

A very special thank you to my sister and travelling companion, Bernadette Spiers, for her patient, enthusiastic assistance; to Ruth and Bob Hamilton, and Eileen and Lew Fell who looked after my children whilst I was away on my journey.

First published 1985 in Great Britain by
Bracken Books, a division of Bestseller Publications Limited,
Brent House, 24 Friern Park, North Finchley, London N12 9DA

in conjunction with
Selectabook Ltd., Hopton Court, London Road, Devizes, Wiltshire

ISBN 0 946495 55 6

Printed and bound in Yugoslavia by Grafoimpex, Zagreb.

Design by Neysa Moss

Contents

Introduction

How lucky can one be! My publisher's brief was to rent a campervan and wander around England painting and sketching anything that caught my eye. I arrived in early spring and stayed until late summer and the experience was a unique and beautiful one.

It's hard for any visitor to assimilate and put on paper even a small proportion of the impressions gathered on a journey such as this. I do know that on many occasions I saw things that the local residents, through sheer familiarity, hardly noticed any more. I hope my book will delight, and bring back fond memories to any visitor to England. And, perhaps, remind all those lucky people who live in so lovely a land, that an unbelievable heritage of beauty surrounds them.

I'm a flower painter principally and make no apologies for filling my book with the glorious blooms that were all around me. Where possible, I have coupled them with a sketch of a building. The individual flowers may not always have grown in, or around, the subject of the sketch, but they were always close by. The paintings are not in strict seasonal sequence, nor do they follow exactly our route around England for they have been arranged to complement each other, and to create a harmonious impression of the whole country. I'm sure the reader will forgive me this small artistic licence.

A golden haze of daffodils, heralding the spring in Windsor Great Park, provides an unforgettable experience for anyone seeing the parks and gardens of England for the first time.

Many English poets, including Shakespeare and Wordsworth, have celebrated the beauty of the daffodil. So did the prophet Mohamet in the first century AD:

> *Let him who hath two loaves sell one, and buy flower of narcissus*
> *For bread is but food for the body, whereas narcissus is food for the soul.*
>
> Mohamet

Windsor Great Park, Windsor, Berkshire.

DAFFODILS *(Narcissus pseudonarcissus)*

Known as "The Painted Lady of the Cotswolds", the village of Broadway with its distinctive Cotswold stone buildings and attractive gardens lining the long main street, must look today much as it did 400 years ago.

The surrounding meadows, turfy downs, woodlands and valleys are alive with Nature's beautiful summer picture of patterns — mullein, rock rose, campanula, agrimony, woodsorrel and willow herb.

I sketched and painted the wisteria, said to be 150 years old, which decorates Old Wisteria Cottage, itself 400 years old.

Wisteria Cottage, Broadway, Worcestershire.

WISTERIA — 150-year-old wisteria outside the 400-year-old cottage.

For over three hundred years botanists and taxonomists have debated the correct name for the little blue flower that carpets the English woodland glades just as the trees break into leaf. The bluebell, also known as the English Hyacinth, has had many curious popular names including griggles, jacinth, cuckoo's boots and crowtoes.

Today the name Endymion, (the woodland lover of the huntress, Diana) is recommended in the Royal Horticultural Society dictionary supplement but learned debate on a flower's origin is not for me. I have simply painted a bluebell tinted glade in a Surrey wood — I think for many this is an English spring.

English Woodland Scene

ENGLISH BLUEBELLS *(Endymion non-scriptus)*

I stepped into my first English garden in Farnham, and was greeted by this mass of delicate pink clematis covering a fence and twining the post of a battered bird-house inhabited by a family of bluetits. A cheeky robin hopped around on the grass.

Farnham, Surrey

CLEMATIS MONTANA "ELIZABETH"

Many of the ancient buildings of Exeter were destroyed by bombs in 1942, but the great Norman Cathedral of St Mary and St Peter survived, despite severe damage. By its 600th anniversary, celebrated in 1969, it had been lovingly repaired and, since then, further restoration has made it one of the most colourful and warmest cathedrals in the kingdom. It was fitting that I should find these rich, velvet textured pansies growing in window boxes in the Close.

The Choir Chancel, Exeter Cathedral, Devonshire.

PANSIES *(Viola wittrockiana)*

Steeped in history, and immortalized by Gilbert and Sullivan in the *Pirates of Penzance*, Penzance, in Cornwall, is the most westerly of English towns. It nestles on the shores of Mounts Bay, which is dominated by the fairytale castle and priory of St Michael's Mount. Local folk lore, legend and rhyme, tell tales of smuggling, shipwrecks, mermaids and Piskies, a Cornish good luck fairy can be seen everywhere — as charms and on gates and statues.

Enjoying a mild climate, the National Trust Morab and Trengwainton Gardens are amongst the most beautiful in the country. Palm, banana and acacia trees, tropical plants and the lovely yellow-flowered New Zealand kowhai, all thrive here far from their native homes.

Penzance, Cornwall

KOWHAI — *(Sophora microphylla)*
BEDDING DAHLIA

These old engine houses and their stacks, mellowed by time and nature, are a reminder of Cornwall's industrial past. They are often overgrown with an abundance of wild flowers carpeting the dunes and transforming cliffs into magnificent natural rock gardens.

Engine-house of the old Giew Mine, between St Ives and Nancledra

FOXGLOVE *(Digitalis purpurea)*
TREE LUPIN *(Lupinus arboreus)*
CREEPING BUTTERCUP *(Ranunclus repens)*

The floral emblem of Bristol since medieval times, the scarlet "Flower of Bristowe", also known as The Maltese Cross or nonsuch, was brought to England by merchants returning from eastern Mediterranean lands when Bristol was Bristowe.

I was fascinated by this street lamp standing outside the Corn Exchange.

Old Street Lamp: Corn Street, Bristol, Avon

THE FLOWER OF BRISTOWE *(Lychnis chalcedonica)*

Garden owners are such a generous breed! By invitation I gathered these during an evening stroll through Honiton, one of the gateways to Devon. I used the ancient town as a base from which to explore neighbouring villages and countryside, and was fascinated by its famous Honiton lace, pottery and buildings like this very old flour mill which, until 25 years ago, had been in constant use for generations.

Old Mill Wheel: Honiton, Devon

CALENDULA *(C. officinalis)*
CARNATION *(Dianthus caryophyllus)*
SWEET WILLIAM *(Dianthus barbatus)*
LOVE-IN-A-MIST *(Nigella damascena)*
EVENING PRIMROSE *(Oenothera missouriensis)*

Following the blossom trail in mid-May through the orchards of Kent, past apple trees laden with delicate fluffy blossom growing round about the unusual, funnel shaped oast houses, is one of my fondest memories. Beauty and history are closely interwoven here as many of the orchards were first planted by the Romans alongside the vineyards they established. Later, these dry, nutty apples were munched whilst supping port wine, but today's taste demands sweeter varieties such as the Cox's Orange Pippin.

Old Oast-House,
Tunbridge Wells,
Kent

"BRAMLEY'S SEEDLING"
APPLE BLOSSOM

Canterbury, the Mother Church of England, famed for its Archbishopric, its Tales, and the murder of Thomas à Becket, stands like a sentinel in the Kent countryside. An old and revered place with an atmosphere rather different to other cathedrals I visited — somehow more venerate, more sacrosanct.

These lovely Marguerite daisies seemed to epitomise my feelings.

The Central Tower: Canterbury Cathedral, Kent

MARGUERITE DAISY *(Chrysanthemum leucanthemum)*

I spent an interesting morning exploring the old buildings of Symondstone Farm at Churt in Surrey. Originally oast-houses, the towers have been removed and they are now barns, partially overgrown with many varieties of wild flower making them particularly attractive.

I stopped at nearby Sandstone House to enquire about an old hayrack I had spotted and, to my delight, was shown around one of the prettiest gardens imaginable. That most beautiful blue climber, clematis, was in full bloom and the fluffy pink weigela was a mass of flowers.

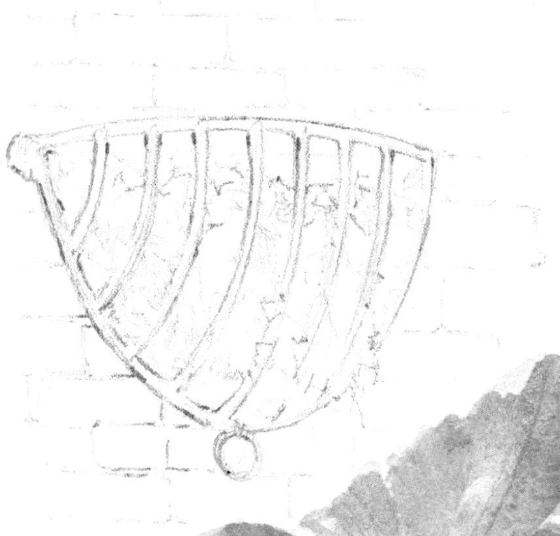

Old Hayrack, Sandstone House, Churt

CLEMATIS *(Clematis jackmanii)*
WEIGELA *(Weigela florida)*

Old Buildings, Symondstone Farm, Churt, Surrey

Sanford Lock, Sandford-on-Thames, Oxford

NASTURTIUM *(Tropaeolum minus)*

I loved the tranquillity of walking in England. Such a contrast to the bush walks of my native New Zealand. On a beautiful sunny day in Oxfordshire when it seemed that every flower, bee and butterfly was out to greet the sun, I started at the busy Sanford Lock on the River Thames. Nasturtiums in the neatly kept gardens reminded me how, as children, we would pick one of the leaves with a drop of dew nestling in the centre, and see how far we could run without losing the dewdrop from the leaf.

I followed the river bank, lingering to watch the brilliant blue and green dragonflies, past fields of cows, horses and docile bulls, to the outer streets of the city of Oxford, where the gardens were ablaze with colour, and finally through the splendid Italianate gateway of the Botanic Garden. Truly a walk to remember.

Italianate Gateway, Botanic Garden, Oxford

DAY LILY *(Hemerocallis citrina)*

The hedgerows of England are an unmatched world of pleasure and interest. Varying in form from rambling stone walls in Cornwall and northern England, to high turfed banks in Devon, hedge lines of holly in Staffordshire, hawthorn in the east Midlands, the Osier willows of Somerset and the tall pines of north-west Suffolk and south-west Norfolk, each has its individual charm.

I was fascinated not only by the wild flowers and creepers, but by the myriad of small creatures living in the hedgerows; butterflies, bees, dragonflies and countless other winged insects balance on leaf, petal and warm bark in the sun whilst, in the undergrowth below, birds, hedgehogs and tiny mice forage, seemingly oblivious to me as I paint and sketch.

Now summer is in flower and natures hum
Is never silent round her sultry bloom
Insects as small as dust are never done
Wie glittering dance and reeling in the sun
And green wood fly and blossom-haunting bee
Are never weary of their melody.

John Clare
The Shepherd's Calendar

LORDS AND LADIES *(Arum maculatum)*
GERMANDER SPEEDWELL *(Veronica chamaedrys)*
FIELD ROSE *(Rosa arvensis)*
RED CAMPION *(Silene dioica)*
TUFTED VETCH *(Dicia cracca)*
COMFREY *(Synphytum officinale)*

For all its remarkable history, and the beauty of its buildings, it is the floral displays in Bath that have remained uppermost in my mind.

Like most visitors, my imagination was stimulated by the Roman Baths and I could see the centurions, the merchants and their ladies, using the elaborate system of spring water and steam for their therapeutic benefit. I pictured the crowning of Edgar, the first King of England, towards the end of the tenth century in the original Abbey built by the Saxons. What a proud setting for the contrasting colours of the fuchsia, petunia, geranium, hydrangea, pansies and the multitude of other flowers displayed in gay hanging baskets, pole gardens, window boxes and tubs.

Pole Garden, Stall Street, Bath

FUCHSIA "PINK QUARTET"

Roman Baths

FUCHSIA "BERNADETTE"

Known in England as "the glory of the garden in June", called by the Chinese "Sho-Yo" (the beautiful), artists the world over have tried to capture the delicate appeal of the peony. I saw this one in Newbridge.

PEONY "SARAH BERNHARDT"

The day I visited Weston Manor (now a hotel) in Oxfordshire, a grand summer fête was in progress. Around the end of the eighteenth century the grounds were laid out by a pupil of "Capability" Brown who replaced the formal gardens of the original eleventh century manor with natural landscaping. They were decorated with topiary hedges, hydrangeas, "Frencham" rose beds, herbaceous borders and ornamental garden pots overflowing with pelargoniums and geraniums.

Weston Manor Hotel, Weston-on-the-Green, Oxfordshire

IVY-LEAVED GERANIUM *Pelargonium peltatum*
PELARGONIUM "REGAL" *Pelargonium domesticum form*
PINK HORSESHOE GERANIUM *Pelargonium zonale form*

When I picked my first "live" field poppy, growing by the roadside in the beautiful Vale of Evesham in Gloucestershire, memories flooded back of my first piece of embroidery, a pattern of red poppies and stalks of golden wheat. A little further on I was greeted with a magnificent view of field after field of glorious red poppies growing amongst wheat.

A few days later, I chanced across the origin of the delightful little corn dollies I had seen everywhere. The corn goddess, a life giving spirit, is said to have hidden in the last sheaf of corn when the field was harvested. The sheaf was kept in the farmhouse over winter and an idol, or dolly, was made from it. The following spring the dolly containing the spirit was broken up and scattered in the fields so the corn would grow and produce a good harvest. The dollies are still made today, though smaller and more elaborate, but the belief lingers on that they bring plenty and good fortune.

Vale of Evesham, Gloucestershire

FIELD POPPY *Papaver Rhoeas*
CORN DOLLY

In the market square at Stow-on-the-Wold I sketched these stocks. Cromwell held nearly a thousand Royalist troops prisoner here after the battle of Stow in 1646 and throughout the middle ages the place was a centre for the wool industry and a large stock-market. Doubtless, the stocks were well used. Today you can try them for size without fear of being delayed on your journey!

I saw the bright flowers of an everlasting pea nearby and it seemed so right — flowers and history everlasting.

Stocks at Stow-on-the-Wold, Gloucestershire

EVERLASTING PEA *(Lathyrus latifolious)*

The local saying, "Stow-on-the-Wold, where the wind blows cold" was far from the truth on the clear, hot, sunny day I was there. Adorned with pretty summer flowers, the entrance to the Parkdene Hotel attracted me. I was intrigued by the 120 year old grape vine, growing in the restaurant beneath its glass ceiling. It always surprised me to see grapes thriving in England and to know they have grown there for over a thousand years.

Parkdene Hotel, Stow-on-the-Wold, Gloucestershire.

GRAPE VINE

Behind this half-timbered, wattle and daub house in Stratford-upon-Avon, lies a very special garden, "Shakespeare's Birthplace Garden". This great English poet frequently used flowers to illustrate his characters. Flowers common in the sixteenth century grow here.

What's in a name? That which we call a rose
By any other word would smell as sweet . . .
Romeo and Juliet, 11,2

Shakespeare's Birthplace. Stratford-upon-Avon, Warwickshire

GOLDEN WINGS (*"Soeur Thérèse"* × (*R. spinosissima altaica* × *"Ormiston Roy"*)

In the ancient town of Appleby-in-Westmorland, stands this tall Georgian "White House" with its interesting ogee headed windows. Hidden behind the busy main street and bordering the River Eden, is one of the most attractive and tranquil gardens I found. The lawns were ready for summer croquet; tall copper beech trees, candytuft and, amongst many other flowers, this lovely Japanese anemone, provide another link with Roman times. Dioscorides, a botanist in the time of Emperor Nero, listed it in his *Codex Vindobonensis*, now one of the rarest books in the world. The viola, or horned violet from the Pyrenees, which has also grown in English gardens for centuries, complemented the anemone's pale beauty.

The "White House", Appleby-in-Westmorland, Cumbria

JAPANESE ANEMONE *(Anemone japonica)*
VIOLA *(Viola cornuta)*

The thatch of "Rose Cottage" first caught my eye, then the flowers — sweet rocket, campanula, long stemmed red roses, ivy and rambling rose, peeping over the picket fence and climbing the walls. A family home in the tiny village of Halford, it is cared for lovingly and kept faithfully in traditional condition, like so many others I saw.

Rose Cottage, Halford, Shipston-on-Stour, Warwickshire

Built as a summer house, this quaint 17th-century rough-stone structure, "Bridge House" is now a tourist information centre. Surely the nursery rhyme, "The Old Woman who lived in a Shoe" was written with this little house in mind? Be that true or not, I was told that a woman with a very large family did, indeed, live there once upon a time. . . .

On a walk to Stockghyll Force Waterfall, nearby, I found this native balsam or touch-me-not, and white clover in full bloom.

Bridge House, Ambleside, Lake District, Cumbria

TOUCH-ME-NOT *(Impatiens noli-tangere)*
WHITE CLOVER *(Trifolium repens)*

From 1799 to 1807 Dove Cottage, in the beautiful Lake District, was the home of the poet William Wordsworth. According to George, who tends the garden now with such loving care, it is still much the same today as it was then. Poppies decorated the garden wall and the wild strawberries from the garden were delicious!

It was originally an Inn called THE DOVE AND OLIVE-BOUGH and Wordsworth with his sister, Dorothy, his wife and three of his five children, spent eight of the happiest years of his life there and wrote of it:

Where once the Dove and Olive-Bough,
Offered a greeting of good ale,
To all who entered Grasmere Vale;
and called on him who must depart,
To leave it with a jovial heart;
There, where the Dove and Olive-Bough
once hung, a poet harbours now,
A simple, water-drinking bard . . .

Wordsworth, *The Waggoner* 1806

Dove Cottage, Grasmere, Lake District, Cumbria

WELSH POPPY *(Meconopsis cambrica)*
WILD STRAWBERRY *(Fragaria vesca)*

It seemed appropriate to find spear thistle growing at the base of the most spectacular relic of Roman Britain — Hadrian's Wall — both appear indestructible! The wall was used in the defence of Roman Britain for over 250 years and is now only a century or so away from being two thousand years old — farmers have fought thistle for as long! This piece of wall is at Walltown Craggs, a typically descriptive English place name, as so many are.

Not far from the spear thistle I painted the harebells, Scottish ones as distinct from English bluebells.

Hadrian's Wall — Section at Walltown Craggs

SPEAR THISTLE
(Cirsium vulgare)
HAREBELLS (Scottish bluebells)
(Campanula rotundifolia)

Beside the river Tyne, Corbridge is one of the most picturesque and historic Northumbrian villages. By the end of the thirteenth century it was a thriving centre for millers, weavers, tailors and goldsmiths, having developed steadily from the end of Roman settlement at the nearby site of Corstopitum, where the famous sculptured lion fountainhead was found. Growing in the old water pump in the town centre were these cheery little French marigolds.

Plaque on pump reads:
Erected by Hugh Percy, Duke of Northumberland
ANNO MD CCXV

Corbridge Lion

FRENCH MARIGOLD *(Targetes patula* — after the Etruscan god Tages, the son of Jupiter)

These roses were growing just outside the city. The rose has long been a symbol used in art, literature and heraldry. The white rose was the heraldic emblem of the House of York, and the red that of Lancaster. Henry VII united the white rose of the House of York with the red of Lancaster to create the Tudor rose, still the royal emblem of England today. The rose has also been used in ecclesiastical architecture and I marvelled at the elaborate, intricate rose window in the Minster, one of the finest in Europe. In the Chapter House an inscription reads:

> *Ut rosa flos florum sic est domus domorum*
> (As the rose is the flower of flowers, this
> is the house of all houses.)

The Shambles, York, Yorkshire

ROSA × ALBA SEMI-PLENA
PAULS SCARLET CLIMBER

Thirsk, a charming North Yorkshire town, was probably inhabited by stone and bronze age man, and visited by Romans who travelled through it to York. In 1755, the founder of Lords cricket ground was born there and more recent fame came when veterinarian author James Herriot used Thirsk as the model for Darrowby in his popular books and television series.

The busy cobblestone market place is dominated by the town clock, erected in 1896 to mark the marriage of the Duke of York to Princess Mary of Teck.

Enjoying the country atmosphere just out of the town, I tasted the first blackberries of the season.

Town Clock, Thirsk, North Yorkshire

BRAMBLE *(Rubus fruticosus)*

Half way between Thirsk and Upsall I found Nevison Hall, the occasional residence of highwayman William Nevison, or "Swift Nick" as he was nicknamed by Charles II because of his particularly skilful horsemanship.

Now unoccupied, the old house has been left to the peaceful intrusion of nature. The door has the date 1666 chiselled below the sculptured horseshoe above the lintel and somehow I felt its history was incomplete. Perhaps its task now is to provide a suitable setting for the weeds or wild flowers which are such a lovely feature of the English countryside — even though my first encounter with a nettle was a little unfriendly! But still I painted one and the butterfly which seemed to like it too.

Nevison Hall, Yorkshire

STINGING NETTLE *(Urtica dioica)*
SMALL TORTOISESHELL BUTTERFLY *(Aglais urticae)*

Early gladioli were making their summer début as I came into Leicestershire, the lovely "gladiolus D'Artagnan" amongst them.

Loughborough has an international reputation for bell casting, and one of the many famous bells cast there was "Great Paul" of St Paul's Cathedral in London. The tower, in Queen's Park, is 150 feet high and houses a carillon of 47 bells; it was built as a memorial to the men of the town who died in the First World War.

The Carillon Tower, Queen's Park, Loughborough, Leicestershire

GLADIOLUS D'ARTAGNAN

As I approached the odd shape of the tall, twisted spire of St Mary and All Saints Church in Chesterfield, I noticed the sunlight catching the beautiful white, wax-like flowers of a madonna lily. It was one of the most spectacular sights I have seen.

Only one other flower, the rose, has received more acclaim in literature than the lily. A paragon of beauty, purity and scent, the exquisite madonna lily has been growing in gardens throughout the world for more than 3,000 years.

Twisted Spire. St Mary and All Saints Church, Chesterfield, Derbyshire

MADONNA LILY *(Lilium candidum)*

"Well-dressing" has long been a form of thanksgiving for a clean and continuous supply of water. The first recorded ceremony took place in Tissington in 1350. Pictures of biblical, local and topical significance were made from flower petals, leaves and other natural materials and set in boards of clay which were used to decorate the wells. In Stoney Middleton, I came across "well-dressing Sunday" being celebrated. A children's flower service had been held in the unusually shaped octagonal parish church and the streets were dressed with bunting.

Stoney Middleton, Derbyshire

CHRYSANTHEMUM *(Chrysanthemum indicum)*
MEADOW CRANESBILL *(Geranium pratense)*
SHASTA DAISY *(Chrysanthemum maximum)*

Parish Church, Stoney Middleton

The custom of "setting the watch" by sounding a horn at each corner of the obelisk in the market square of Ripon continued without a break for over 1000 years. It indicated to the inhabitants that they were in the care of the "Wakeman" for the night. I have drawn the Wakeman's House, built in the 14th century.

Bindweed was growing beside the carpark and I could not resist painting the trumpet shaped flowers and glossy leaves.

Wakeman's House, Market Square, Ripon, Nr. York

HEDGE BINDWEED *(Calystegia Sepium)*

A weaver called Hill and his family started carving this unusual "house" out of, or into, the cliff overlooking the River Nido in 1770.
I was given a delightful posy of harebells picked from the top terrace garden.

Hill the Weaver must have been inspired by John the Mason, who 362 years before in 1408, completed The Chapel of Our Lady of the Crag. Hewn out of the same solid rock, it must be the most unusual chapel in all England. John was granted a licence to build it by Henry IV and carved the figure of a knight to guard the entrance.

The Mock Orange was growing in a nearby churchyard, reminding me of the real orange blossom in my garden at home.

Knaresborough, Yorkshire

MOCK ORANGE BLOSSOM
(Philadelphus coronarius)
HAREBELLS *(Campanula rotundifolia)*

Warm, late afternoon air was laden with the scent of lavender as I approached Caley Mill Lavender Farm near King's Lynn in Norfolk. No wonder, for the softly glowing shades of purple flowering plants carpeted the fields for as far as the eye could see.

A native of the Alpine regions of the Mediterranean coast, it is believed the Romans introduced lavender to England as a bath scent. Today, English lavender is popular worldwide and much is grown and processed at the early nineteenth century Caley Mill, which replaced an earlier mill, one of those recorded in the Domesday Book in the "Vill" of Heacham.

Caley Mill, Heacham, King's Lynn, Norfolk

LAVENDER Nana 1. *(Atropurpurea)*

The first castle at Windsor was built by William the Conqueror over 900 years ago but the existing buildings date from the fourteenth century. These hollyhocks, growing tall and proudly against the Horseshoe Cloister, were the first flowers I saw within the ancient walls which have provided protection and a home for Royal families since the twelfth century.

Windsor Castle, Windsor, Berkshire

HOLLYHOCKS *(Althaea)*

If I was granted
a single wish for
fellow flower lovers
I would ask that
they could visit the
magnificent gardens of the
Royal Horticultural Society at Wisley. Massing
together in a spectacular display of colour and
design, the last of the azaleas and rhododendrons,
together with herbaceous border and rock garden
plants of bewildering variety, gave me the
impression of an enormous, richly woven persian
carpet — perhaps a magic one to make my wish
come true!

This lovely old house is the Royal Horticultural Society
Headquarters and although a working building it commands
attention, layered with a dozen different creepers, apparently
mellow on the outside but alive with horicultural research inside. I
think that epitomises the English garden, outwardly quiet and
tranquil but inside pulsating with the vibrant rhythm of nature.

The Laboratory Building, R.H.S. Garden, Wisley

AZALEA "FROME" *(Said to derive from a Saxon phrase meaning "ford of the golden flowers".)*

Broom, though humble today, was highly significant in ancient heraldry. Plantagenet Kings and Queens derived their name from it — Planta genista. Broom is sculptured on the effigy of Richard II in Westminster Abbey, where the coronation of every English Monarch since William the Conqueror, and every British Sovereign since the Union of Crowns, has taken place. No wonder that even the crowds of sightseers cannot dim its aura, which projects you back into history more surely than any science-fiction time machine.

Westminster Abbey, London

BROOM *(Planta genista)*

For years, I had looked forward to visiting Kew Gardens and I was not disappointed.
The Japanese Pagoda was such a contrast to the Palace of Kew that I could not resist a sketch.

Kew Gardens, Richmond

RHODODENDRON "Pink Pearl"

Ashdown Forest once covered more than fourteen thousand acres of the Wealden country of Sussex, Kent and South-west Hampshire. Today a little over six thousand acres survives. From the village of Hartfield I walked a forest track (carefully observing the Forest Code which applies to designated 'areas of outstanding beauty') bordered by flowers, balsam and native orchids, gorse and tall trees, to 'Pooh Sticks Bridge'. Leaning on the rails of the bridge which spans a small stream in a shady clearing, childhood memories of Pooh Bear and Christopher Robin tumbled through my mind.

The memorial stone beside the bridge reads
"Pooh Sticks Bridge
Immortalised by A. A. Milne and Ernest Shepard.
Built in 1902 by J. C. Osman and restored in
1979 by National Westminster Bank and D.L.S
Ltd for East Sussex County Council."

Pooh Sticks Bridge, Hartfield, (Ashdown Forest)

HEATH SPOTTED ORCHID *(Dactylorhiza ericetorum)*
GORSE *(Ulex europaeus)*
INDIAN BALSAM (POLICEMAN'S HELMET) *(Impatiens gladulifera)*

POOH STICKS BRIDGE

I sought wild flowers on a long leisurely walk which took me along the old 'Pilgrims' Way' in Kent. Later, relaxing with friends in their home in Sevenoaks, I had the opportunity to paint in their lovely old world garden, heady with the fragrance of rose, late violet, carnation, lavender, lilac and wallflowers — hence my title for the painting, "Pot-Pourri Garden".

Seven Oaks, Kent

VIOLET *(Viola riviniana)*
YELLOW ROSE *(Marechal niel)*
PINK ROSE *(Pink Favourite)*
CARNATION *(Dianthus chinensis)*
LAVENDER *(Lavendula officinalis)*
LILAC *(Syringa vulgaris)*
WALLFLOWER *(Cheiranthus cheiri)*

One of my last memories at the end of my wanderings is a visit to St Clere's at St Osyth in Essex. The day was perfect and the cottage enchanting.

It was originally built about 1355. The heavy timbers were framed on the ground and then 'reared' into position with the help of the neighbours! A formidable task indeed. Old records show payment of meat and drink to the villagers for their help.

St Clere's, St Osyth, Essex

ROSE 'AUTUMN DELIGHT'
DAFFODIL 'GOLDEN HARVEST'
BORDER IRIS

Our England is a garden that is full of stately views,
Of borders, beds and shrubberies and lawns and avenues, . . .

Rudyard Kipling